At School

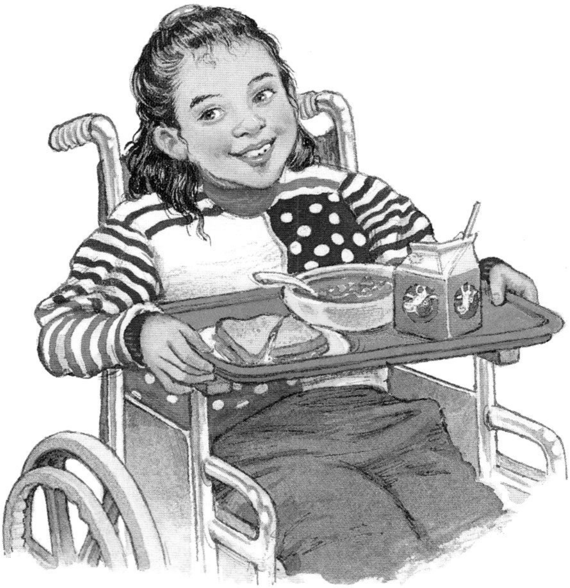

Written by Mary Ann Doyle
Illustrated by Renée Mansfield

Scott Foresman

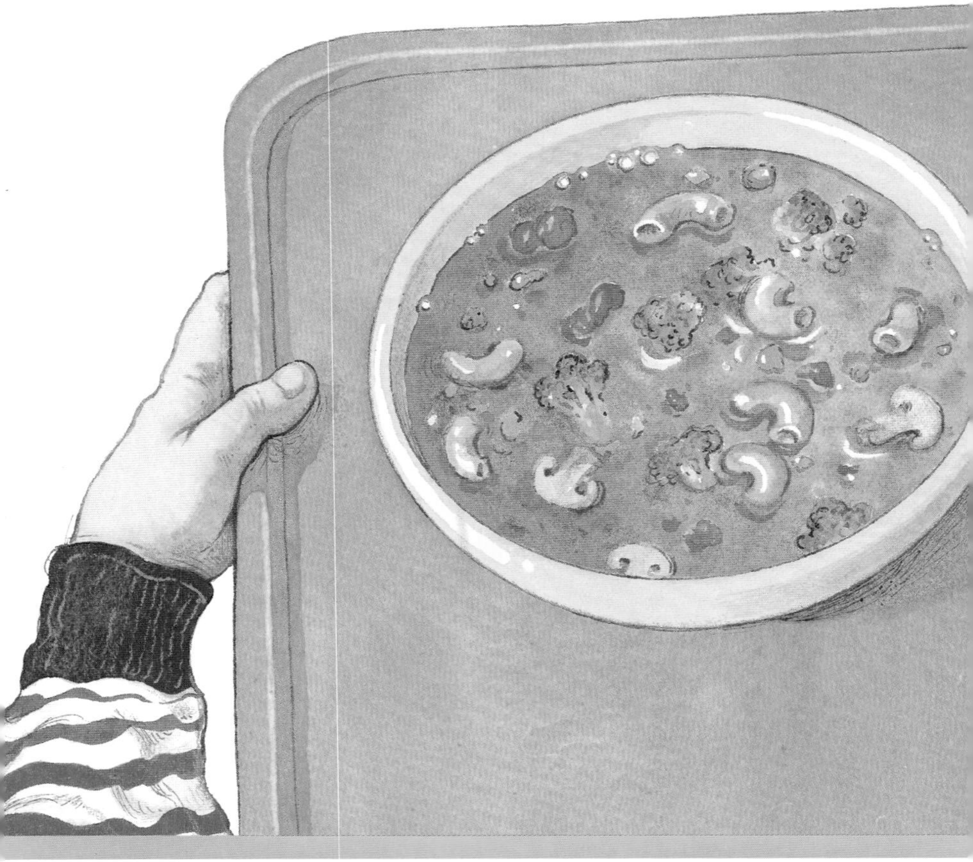

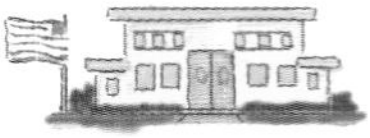 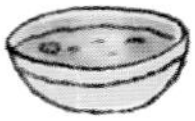

At school, the soup

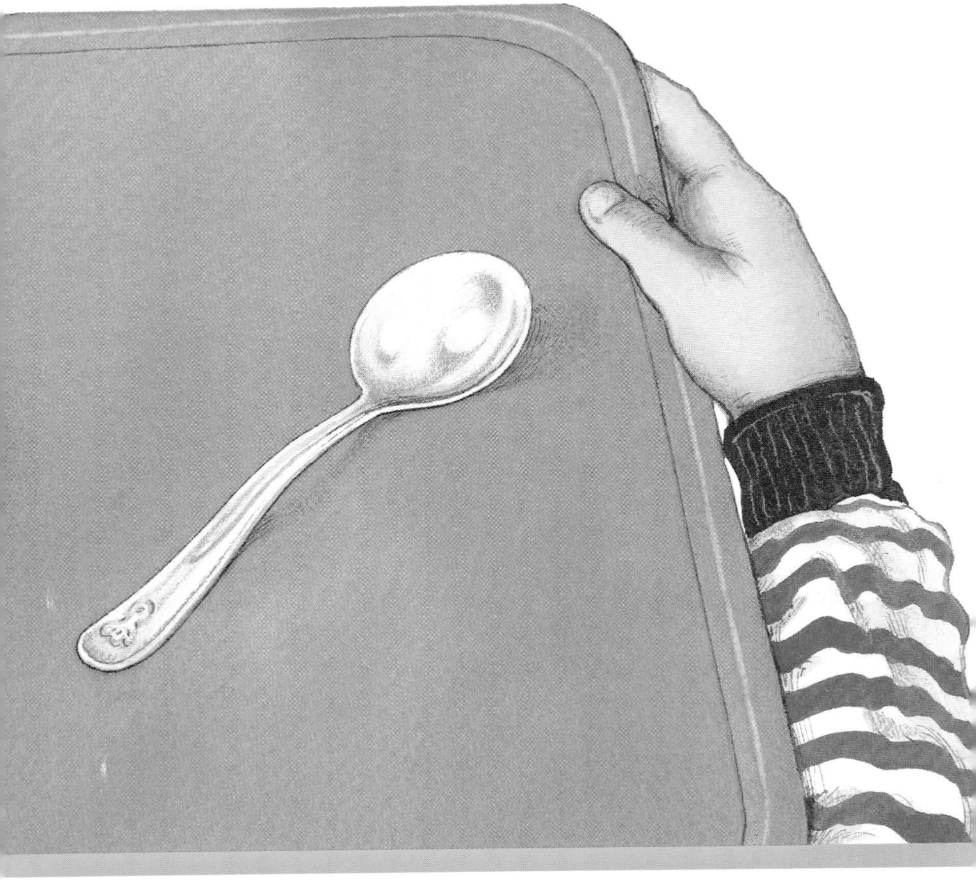

a spoon

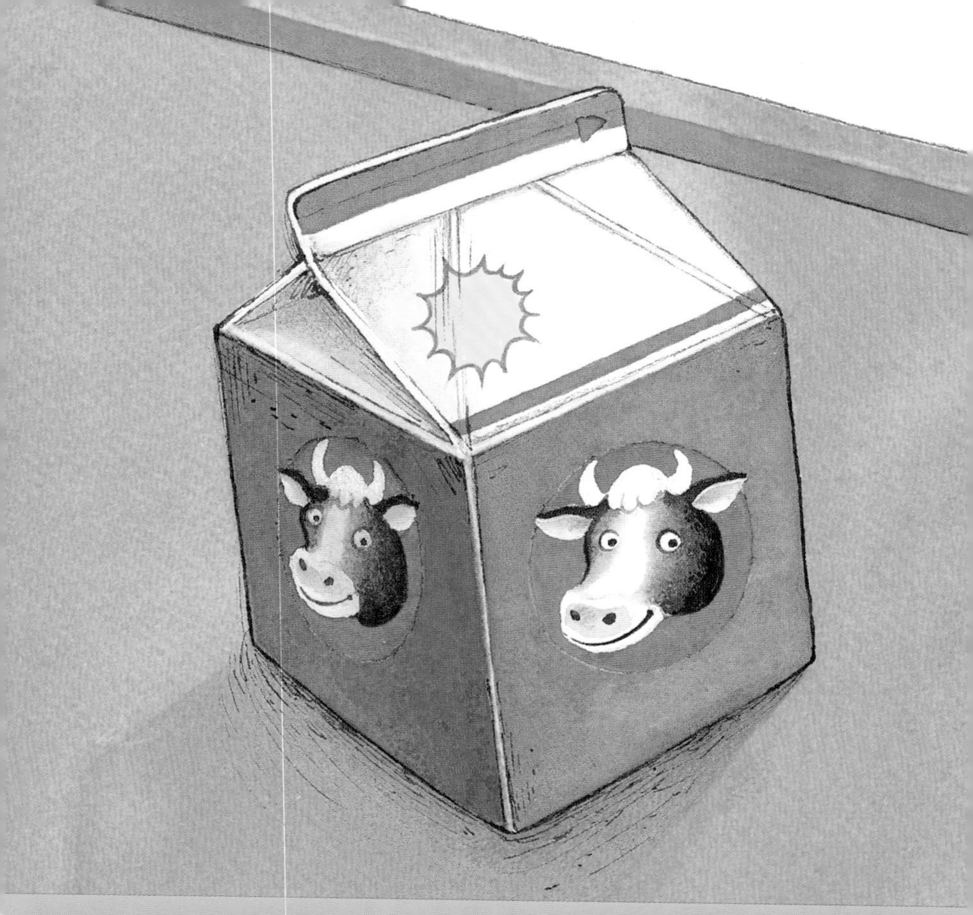

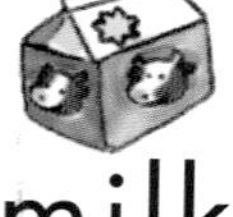

the milk

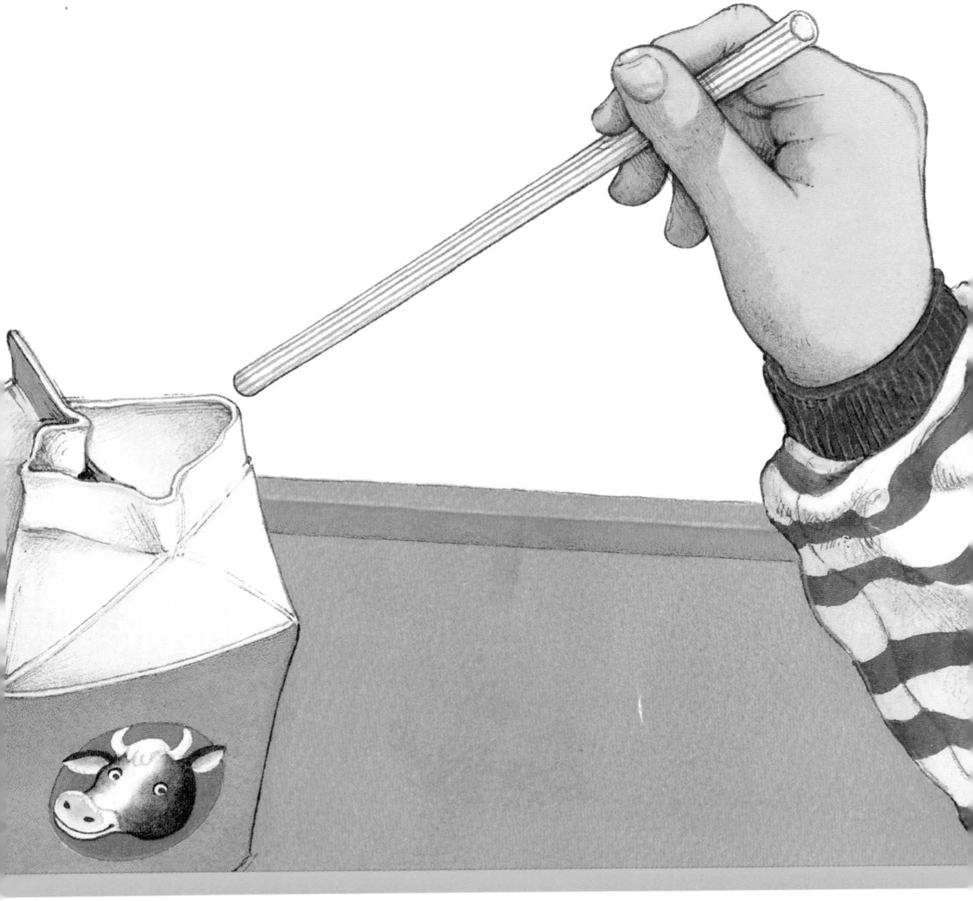

a straw

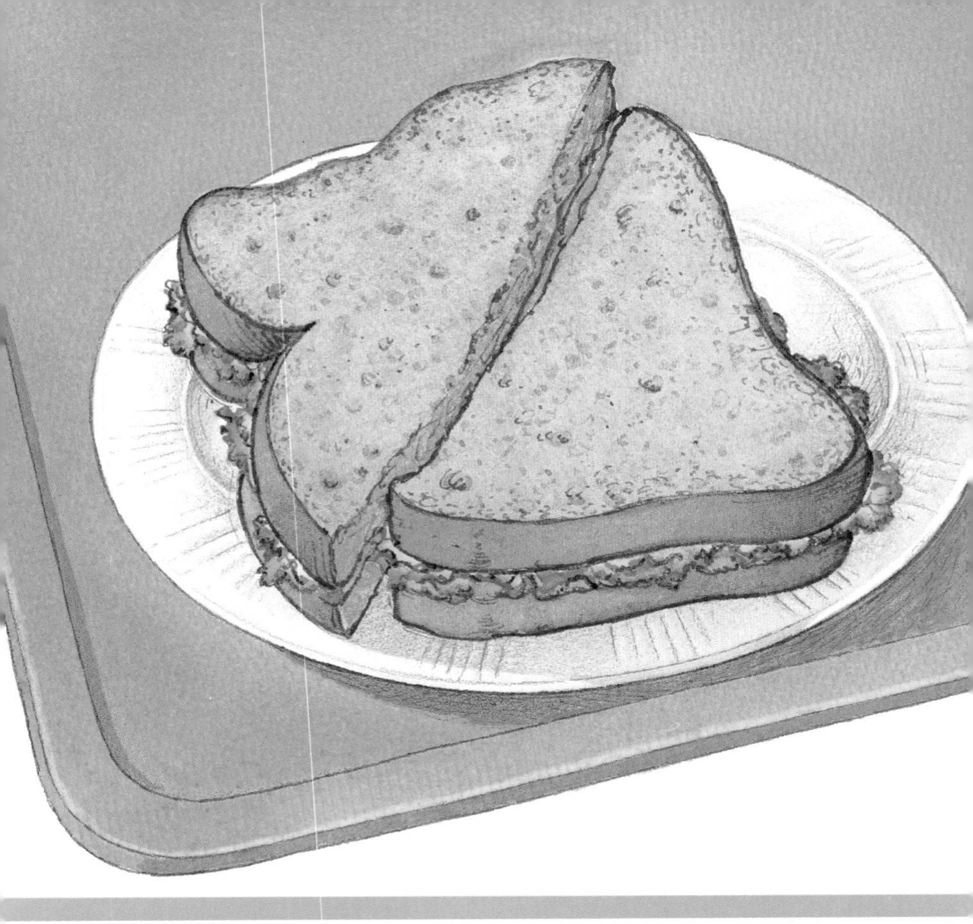

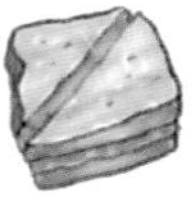

a sandwich

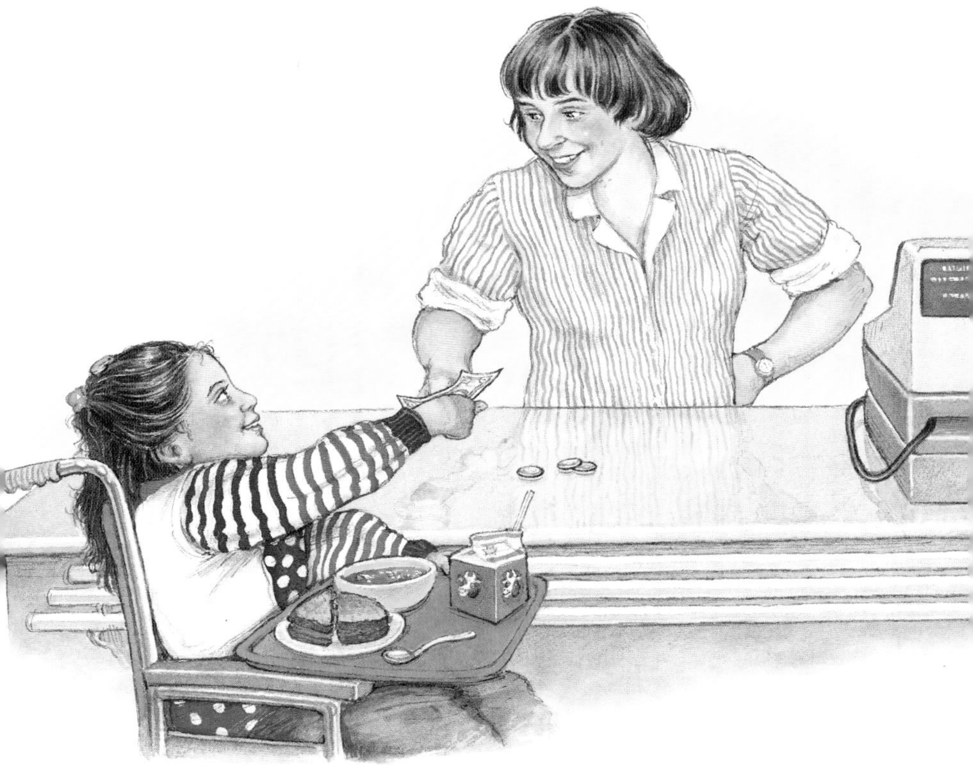

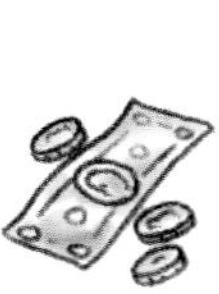

the money

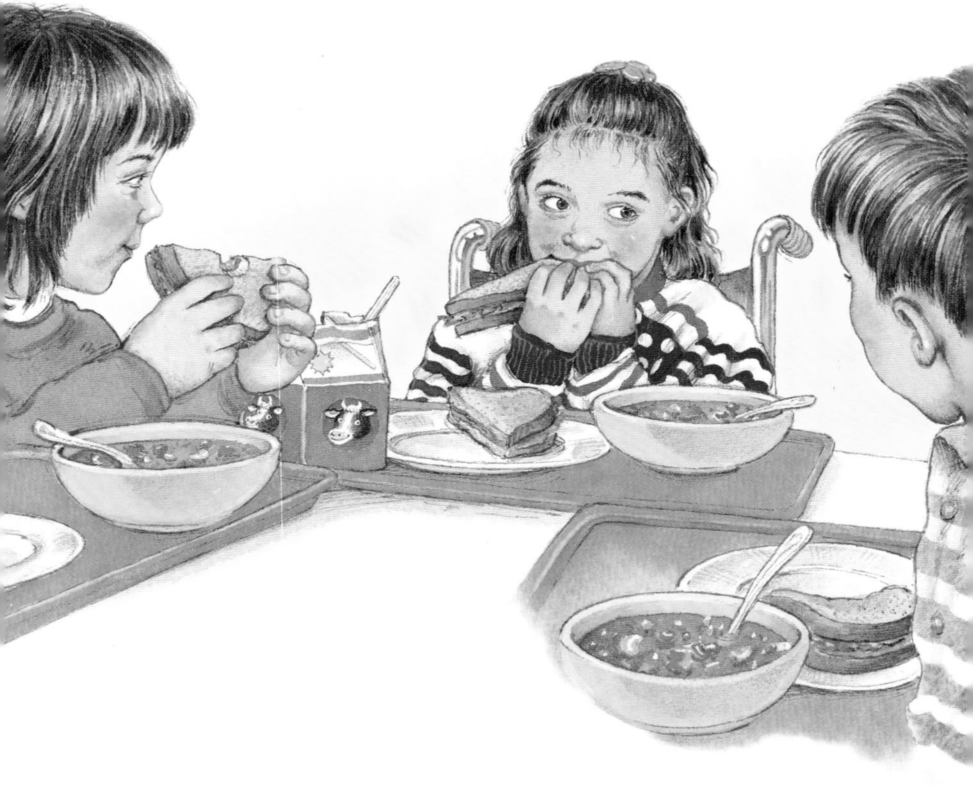

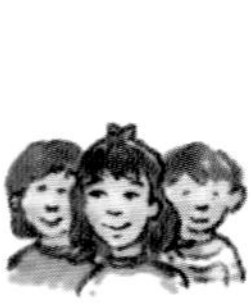 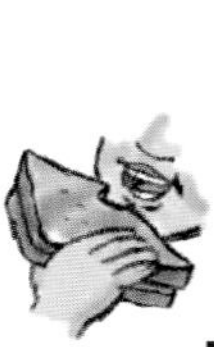

The children can eat!